T5-CCL-486

DISCARD

BLUFF VIEW
from the
TWIN CITIES

by Ron Weber

POEMS FROM THE WEST BANK

Published by

HARBOR HOUSE
P U B L I S H E R S

Harbor House Publishers, Inc., 221 Water Street, Boyne City, Michigan 49712
Manufactured in the United States of America

Library of Congress Cataloging-in-Publication Data.
Weber, Ron, 1946-
Bluff View from the Twin Cities: poems from the west bank / by Ron Weber.
p. cm.
ISBN 0-937360-24-4: $14.95
1. City and town life–Michigan–Poetry. 2. Benton Harbor (Mich.)–Poetry.
3. Saint Joseph (Mich.)–Poetry. I. Title.
PS3573.E224B58 1993
811'.54–dc20
93-27289
CIP

Acknowledgements

I need to acknowledge and thank two individuals in particular relative to this book: Kathy Zerler and Dick Schanze.

Kathy was the first person I bounced the idea off of. Her initial reaction was enthusiastic and very supportive. We talked a few times early in 1993 and her encouragement helped me nurture the idea and develop the book proposal. I think it was in the way she said, "Ron, do it!"

Dick Schanze's backing was instrumental. His review of the project proposal lead to needed refinements in pursuit of additional information. Thanks, Dick. And thanks for the overall support you provide for the arts.

I also wish to thank those magazines and small and university literary publications in which my work has previously appeared for reassigning the publishing rights to me.

Introduction

This collection of poems represents a kaleidoscope of one writer's reactions to this drama we call life. It springs from a midwestern context and the contrasting heritage drawn from being a native of the Twin Cities of Benton Harbor and St. Joseph, Michigan; a community on the west bank nestled in the southwest corner where the St. Joseph River flows into Lake Michigan. Artsfest is a major annual event to celebrate art and artists in this community. The net proceeds from the sale of this book are being donated to that effort.

The "view" in this collection is not just from some local settings, it is also a commentary on the human spirit as it experiences a broad range of universal themes whether on the west bank, the east coast, or along the pacific shore. As you read the poems you will find yourself in many places, some of which you'll define in your own mind. We will go to New York and, at least once, to Vietnam.

You'll be reading, in part, one midwest poet's report on the world around him; introspective, reflective, descriptive and satirical. Tidbits, if you will, shaved from that spectrum of emotions we all find ourselves bumping into periodically as we weave in and out of the decades of our lives.

A final note. A number of poems do have general settings or actual locations within the Twin Cities as a springboard for the piece. They are "Bluff View", "Mendel", "Lunch Alone at Babe's Lounge", "The Fountain", "Eavesdropping", "Milton Street", "Territorial Road and Other Sorrows", "Live from Baskin Robbins", "Main Street Runs", and "Saigon on the Boulevard".

Ron Weber, July 1993

Contents

Short Stories

Present at the Creation

Scripts from unwitting writers ring
In petrified recital as I wait
   as I wait
Rushing nothing in wishing wait away.
Fear forages through memory obscured
By sounds of painful spasms,
Pursuing cues I hoped to know;
Learned and lost to anxious uncertainty
As I recall swelling women
   and doubtful men.

In submission to passionate moments
Months ago, you tremble.
You labor at evolution's art
Molding love into life,
Delivering blue stillness onto an ivory wrap.

Room enough, you beckon.
We listen together
As feeble breath fades the blue.
Infant whimpers begin to sing their song
Through the silence of the antiseptic room.

Report on the Subterranean Bards

They play shuffled bookings
As Jekyll, Hyde, the
Invisible man.
Filtering between
Without being seen
Unless caught by a voyeur,
Or spread across a page
By their own careless hand.
Exposed to those stopping
To hear what they read,
Lives captured by stanzas
In a time-flight filigree.

Flying high doesn't help,
Nor the great olive chase
For those in the race
To the bottom of a glass,
Languishing in a bardic trap.

Biographers to
The olive people,
The tightrope walkers.
They grab at chords
To play us all
In songs we never wrote.
To play us all
And find us there
Hiding between the notes.

Shortfall

Spring took you
On passing along with
Clean rain, fresh smells,
Cool streams from melted snow.

You were May
Molding earth's ornaments
With petal hues, blossom tints;
Sculpturing laughter while
Lightly authoring love
In a single season.

Winds consume
Belated seedlings
Clutching the soil
In desperation.
Spring strives to reach
Across the pause of summer
And learn what autumn knows.

Its been years
From May to August.
I've seen you ever since
In the somnolent illusions
Of midnight.

August seems lost to summer
When everything is over,
There only as a bookmark
Or someone's 40th birthday.

There's a certain fear
When entering autumn
Diverting us with color
While amputating the day
At six o'clock.

There's a certain fear
When days grow short
And you've only lived
In springtime.

Portrait

July's breath drizzles down
Widening to a hot summer yawn.
We lay together on the beach
With Sandburg and Hemingway,
Sipping the sun
To quench the winter's thirst.
I study your profile
As you stare the southern breeze.
Ruffling puffs of wind and shadows
Paint your portrait,
Sketching delicate hair,
Soft features.

I stroke the valley of your back
To play your song again,
To listen to the music
Of your movements as
I kiss your thighs.
Yesterday's concerts strain
To embrace your outline,
Stillborn as I touch nothing.
The sun slowly squints good-bye
While seagulls chant,
Tolling words that rang the end.

At the Bus Stop

Traffic lights blink their
Tenacious pulse at hollow
Intersections disturbed only
Briefly by sporadic motion.
Autos foray through concrete
Canyons to be baptized by
Pigeon waste from sills of
Unwashed windows weeping
Their past.

Carcass pickers move to purge
What remains, appearance
And departure synchronized
In celestial clockwork:
    sunrise,
        sunset.
Remnants of life crumble
Fighting for breath, vomiting
Their fading hope to hang
Statically around us.

Song of a Carpenter
for Albert Berndt

He left one late February eve,
Eight-eight winters were enough.
Too fast that ride from horse-drawn lumber
To space shots,
Microchips.

A builder; artisan caressing nature
With a master's stroke
Molding oak and pine and cedar
Into legacies worth every penny.

He took his solitude in the land.
A planter of crops in the vernal sun
Of each new year,
Furrowing the earth as he tilled
To tuck seeds into nurturing pockets of loam.
And by the moon it was always done.

Summer carried the songs of his saws
As they worked each board
Singing out to the ears of his children.
Evening echoed his work in the harvest soil,
Holding a handful of dirt,
Inhaling the scent of new life
As years pressed on.
He touched the children of his children
With jokes of gentle humor.

An instant montage weaved
Skyscrapers and headstones.
In free-fall your cries
Were captured by innocent air,
Now an accomplice as friction
Silenced you.

Time offered not a blink
When you hit concrete.

Atom Dance

The last blast fades
Softly. A symphony, almost,
Or requiem.
Atoms dance around us parading
Up and down the streets, infiltrating
Borders to shake our hands,
Slap our backs and say
Congratulations.
Kissing babies along the way.

A spider wraps flecks of rust
In his silent shawl; small, weak
Winner that time made king,
With a little help.
It drapes a home from muzzle to stock,
Tiptoeing over us, whistling.
The song throbs in eerie echoe
Accompanied by the hum of twilight.

Blue haze lowers an anointing palm
In a solemn extreme unction,
Stretching on to spread the word.
"Man's museum," breathes the wind
As nightfall shouts "Buy a neon sign!"

Relocation

It only took the morning to move you out.
Doesn't take long when no one's there.
Moved out a few years first,
Then decades.
Didn't take as long as decades might
   . . . time flies.
The house now only a shadow
Of yesterdays.

You hid alot of early years
In places we'll never find
But I know you've got 'em.
It's all the county lets you keep
When it's four to a room
Living in the past,
Inhaling that medical ammonia,
Breathing in each other's excrement.
Invisible keepsakes are all that's allowed
Besides a comb, robe, cards
Taped on the wall.
Invisible keepsakes
Don't take up much space.

A magician delivers visiting hours
Each day—now you see 'em,
   now you don't.
A treasury of hours dwindles
As the bookie of hope takes bets
On tomorrow.

Milton Street

We're lucky we didn't break our legs
Jumping from the porch;
What do children know of luck.
Days of play were all we knew
   all that mattered.

Remember the wild berries we
Picked along the fence for
Pies our mothers would make? Strange
Their smiles in summer-heated kitchens,
But the hard part was the picking
   we were certain of that.

We watched the welders in the
Factory across the street
Fascinated by their eery
Metal masks and
Copying them with sparklers
On the Fourth of July.
Curious to us why they would
Leave such fun so rapidly
At the end of the afternoon.

The old vacant lot is asphalt
Now; cars replaced the weeds.
That tall grass hid our
Adolescence then as we
Reclined to watch the sky
And spoke of serious things,
Asking questions we couldn't answer.
Understanding was in silent moments,
   the unsure touching.

I know now why they left
So rapidly, but I haven't
Watched many clouds glide by
Nor sipped the brandy of sunset
As it spills across the sky.
I haven't lain in tall grass since.
Have you?

Night Talk

With quiet blindness
In the evening void
Soft kissing fingertips tread
Over my thighs, turning my mind
From wasteful slumber.
You draw me to magic movements
Flooding my senses, holding them
Ransom for the same.

A cool night breath intrudes
To nudge your hair across my face,
Thousands of silk fingers
Adding their embrace.
I turn to touch fragrant breasts,
Lower to mold our warmth.
You and darkness blend
To share my love.
Tender passion urges night
To steal the sun.

Encounters and Eavesdropping

Bluff View

Dense grass cools my limbs, tickles my
Ankles bared by sloppy socks, sitting
Back-to-bark on a lush green strip
Of bluff. The jutting sentry overlooks
The foaming bluegreen mix, the channel
Offering solace while passing mid-day.

A siren song still sings slowly
Pulling us through the millennia.
Midshipmen and midwives, merchants
And maidens lay hope, lay sorrow at
The goddess of the sea. A pulse of
Forever is in each thundering beat of
The breakwater, in each nurturing echo
Of eternity.

An old man sits on the edge tolerating
My presence. I'm not sure whether
His glare shouts "Intruder!" or
Simply labels me indifferently.
My wave is wasted. "Hi." Nothing.
"How are you?" The same, a look
Then quickly away.

No aid from spectacles, solid hands
Grasp his only concession to time,
A cane more carried than used.
He departs with a darting glance.
I half smile then turn away, refusing
His steps. The indolent summer day
Shares its warmth with everyone and
Asks no payment for its breeze.

Sunset

You sink hypnotically
To hang suspended at sea line
While gloaming spirits
Play their final game,
Coaxing timid shadows to
Write an epilogue.

You play a sonata of hues
And movement as clouds fade
From the orange eruption,
Spilling your brandy across the sky.
Vermillion tint rides
The marge of twilight to
Peer at sunbirds dancing and
Skipping their reflections
Across the water.

You murmur a hymn
Of flowing pink blending
A saffron chorus in calm repose,
Wrapping the world in apricot ribbon
Before shrouding it in silence
Until morning.

You nurture dusk
With the wink of
Fleeting glimmers that
Kiss the horizon good night.

The Novel

Your moods remind me
Of my periodic self
As I read your pages,
Or you read them to me.

I didn't and don't mind
Listening. My own thoughts
Have broken free to be blown
Through landscapes searching
And seeking their place.

Your middle chapters
Flown in honest writing
Passages more descriptive
Authoring observations of
What is, what might have been.

A fading from the opening
Where feelings were freely
Given, yet stolen by romantic
Fraud unseen by youth,
Only concerned with titles.

Having dabbled myself
I thank you for sharing
The unfinished manuscript.
I'm no literary critic so
I can't offer too much,
Leave that for "The New York Times."

(Was it just a coincidence of time
And place that gained me access?)

The sun doesn't charge
For its warmth so write
The final chapters on the beach.
It's cold and lonely
This time of year, I know.
But summer is on its way.

Lunch Alone at Babe's Lounge

My smile was just a courtesy
Returning yours. Being polite.
Don't take it for anything more.
Believe what you want about
Your pretty face; subtle creases
Its only Judas. Its vintage
Equal to mine.
I turned to the window
To gaze the tumbling river,
My eyes stumbling over yours.
I know what you want—I want;
What we'd give for a drink, idle words,
Whatever else would justify it.

Is it easier now?
Does age play fewer games or
Is loneliness our secret mentor?
Where were you before when I probed
Those fine-line smiles, certain you
Would fold into shallow pockets,
Serve to be my mattress?
What made us think that was so important?

The river runs awesome in autumn
Thrusting out its prewinter chest.
I would turn again for a glimpse
If you weren't there.
The current caresses the bank.
Arms splash around the smallest island,
Hugging it against winter's fate.

Silent Child

From a broken room
The eternal liberation moves
In freedom from twisted people,
Past those watching in whispers
Of love and sorrow too late.
Carried out in a stranger's hug
To an unfelt sun that never knows
When to laugh or cry.

Creeping storms torment the night
As small twigs snap
In eery reverberation,
Disturbing discussions
Of distant disciples
And abortion people
Battling over blurred barricades,
Neither having to write the epitaphs.

Arrival

Silently pursuing, love
Comes gentle in a blind embrace,
Entering unseen against a burning sun.
Its hushed paws of mist-wind
Kiss the bluff to feed
Embryos of spring, leading
A chorus of cottonwoods.

It molds a delicate chain
Stumbling over yesterday's dreams,
Dragging its trunk of unrehearsed dancers
And the uncertain songs
Of tomorrow.

Parable

They never dreamed of being
A midnight writer foraging
In the dusty trunk
Of their subconscious,
Garment bags of awareness
Dotted with foreign stickers
They're still trying to read.

Lettered keys bang against
The carriage to bounce off
Every wall in the place,
Settling on the floor with wads
Of crinkled paper.

They shoot at moving targets;
Contradictions regroup to send in
The calvary to slash their wrists.
They'd do it themselves but
Then what? Hands dropping off to
Leave them in hopeless despair.

Red-blotched papers only
Bring more rejections to
A love affair with
The blank white lady.

Their stare is ceaseless.
She dares them to
Caress her with tenderness
Or outrage and send her off,
With fulfillment.

Biography

They sat too long
With eyes burning
In watery protest.
They would have washed them out

If they could, but the door
Was locked or jammed,
Or something.
A few more dramas,

A wave of sitcoms and
Maybe. . ., shifting around
For hours waiting to
Relieve themselves. They

Refused to clean up the
Pending mess as pictures
Played off blurry faces,
Juggling sound-bites
Between them.

A crowd moved through
Grimaced smiles, canned laughter.
Some booed, hissed, lapsed
Into a sleeping silence. They

Awoke with applause for some
Celluloid feature as they were
Carried out screaming for
Station identification.

Awoke with applause as their
Narrow daydreaming brought
Phantoms humming low and long.

Brought a soft chorus of
Children chanting, chanting now
The executioner's song.

Fade-out in Central Park

A half-a-dozen yesterdays sit
In the dim, wavering silhouette of shade
Staking another claim while they can.
Wind and leaves carry on their conversation
So common they're paid little attention,
Pausing only to catch their breath.
Silent sounds tick off from a sundial
You'll never find.

A half-a-dozen yesterdays are
Talking, walking, gazing intently
At todays strolling by, waving
At tomorrows that play around them.
Playful blinks of life come
Only so close in curiosity, answered
With smiles that fit into memories
Much easier than words.

Day labors to sunset as wind
And leaves break their dialogue;
Words echo in muted evening ambience.
Time secretly whispers by on silent feet
Smiling to itself, planning
A surprise party.

Progressing
for Kurt Vonnegut, Jr.

Do you see it? The light!
We're making it!
I can see we're making it
Through the maze.
Rats in heat cutting corners
To the official, the sanctioned,
Suspended from the wall
Behind neat cut glass
To be dusted, straightened, hung
Just so.

It's been decreed
The world will breathe
In a labyrinth marked off
By five-foot partitions;
The drab wrapper of cubicle man
With cubicle colleagues humming
To a player piano.
Processed people process people.
Taking them
Remaking them
By filling in the blanks,
Recasting them in paper
To prove that they are,
Plugging them into paragraphs
That tell them what's real.

System messiahs save us all
Suspended from the wall
Behind neat cut glass
To be dusted, straightened, hung
Just so.

War Sequels in Time-lapse

You skipped fine features of youth
Down cobbled streets playing
On the threshold of womanhood.
Your face framed an innocence that
Betrayed you when the fatherland
Was finally breached,
Another historical embrace by
The movements of the mighty.

You bowed to the kingdom
On your back to parading emperors,
Collectors of art spreading your thighs
In the nightmare maturing of
Your many uses, and re-uses
In the prostration of your will.
Mechanical now after months of learning
How to smile at the executioner
To keep yourself alive,
To keep you from the hunger
That haunted your birth.

And so your homage to the liberators
Raining in like holy water,
Anointing your soil with the freedom
Of the victor.
Your admiration to the gladiators
As you lie with young men
With desperation in their eyes,
As you lie with their captains
Sketched in aged resignation.
They blend to an ancient image.

From decades that humbled youth
You drag lost destiny
In tattered shawl, faded babushka down
Cobbled streets with
Young men of spent time.
From your gnarled, vanquished soul you
Reach with ruptured eyes for those
Who will keep you from
The movements of the mighty.

Silhouette

The last chance limousine
Yawns to surrender a small
Frail figure. Slow motion
Views quivering effort as she
Emerges in arduous triumph,
Showered in caromming sunlight
Reflected by unironed skin.
Paid in advance by
Legacies of her womb,
The cabman leaves.

She trembles past
White-frocked frauds smiling
A welcome that says good-bye.
Days become too rapid for age
When time embezzles strength.
Pride battles the pale room
Being fed, bathed, walked, groomed.
They severed her hands
Numbed her will,
She passed away.
They'll bury her when she
Stops breathing.

Eavesdropping

Find a table at H. I.'s Saloon
Or most other pubs on the planet.
Order a drink if you laugh
Too seldom or run from yourself
More often than you'd like.
Forget the "Happy Hour" distortions
And listen in the lateness to those
There because there's nowhere else.

Dr. Jekyll pours a jigger of therapy.
You dissect your mind in the
Only honest place in town
Besides a confessional. But there's
No draft on tap at church.

Fragments of joy, shrapnel of sorrow
Bounce around the room to be grabbed
By collectors like loose change.
I've shared more people than know me
Collecting donations of joy and sorrow,
Wondering what contribution will be mine.

Saturday Show

Down the midway nudges
The shifting flow
Climate controlled,
All under one roof.
Mall walk, mall talk
Stealing away the day
With contemporary amusements.
A peep show and
A freak show weave
From shop to shop as
Thin clad breasts jiggle free
Below fine-skinned faces,
And distant young men with
An earring or two, or three;
Varied groups claiming their turf.
The crude play the sophisticate
Not really knowing how.
The sophisticated know they are,
They don't stay long.

A squat, tattered woman slowly
Leads her brood from side show
To side show letting them laugh
And run and shout.
Plaster people display the
Latest styles she
Can never buy.

Five giant pretzels are
A Saturday lunch as
She tells the children she can't
Make up her mind which dress
To buy. . .So it goes.
The youngest steals
A pack of play money.
She's going to give it all away
On the playground.

Interlude at the Englewood Motel

A little too early, maybe.
The eleventh hour still leaves
A piece of the day.
Hope spills its potion;
A snake oil for sentient slumber.
Daydreams do their striptease behind
Blank stares and pensive eyes,
A sly set of handcuffs you don't
Even feel.

But she fooled 'em tonight,
Cut 'em loose. Traded 'em in
For a permanent fix.
Pulled one on all of us, ya know,
Knocking around in that bogus
Body of dreams,
Making us feel she was real.

Trying to buy-off those midnight
Movies broke the bank
That never was.
In kinship with Norma Jean
She turned off the lights,
Pulling the shade with
A steel hand, counting shots
For a diversion before
She hit the floor.

American Profile and Other Ballads

American Profile

You've grown more stubborn, stumbling
Furtively through the neighborhood,
Following me home.
I thought I left you miles back.
You dart across the street riding
The wind, hiding
In shrubs, wrapping around posts
And trees.
Empty bags, plastic cups, vacated
Sacks of fries decorate the land
In tenacious pursuit.

You're even seductive winking
And blinking with neon eyes.
"Come on in you finger lickin',
Extra large, he-man, all the salad
You can eat son-of-a-gun."
Dive into the din of the crowd
Singing the Slop Shop Serenade.
A quarter poundered-
Secret ingrediented-
Kentucky fried reflection
With running water and
A toilet indoors.
   Mind if I use it?

Morning

The day drips relentlessly
Akin to that Chinese torture
But painless.
Uncomfortable
Inconvenient
Essential to evicting me
From slumber's sanctum.
But I'm glad it's the sun.
It brings winged singers
To serenade my shave
And whistle with me while I dress.
A dependable friend
For even in the winter stillness
You hear the birds you thought
Had long since left
Singing from places you cannot find.

I leave to do the day
By turning away the question marks.
I need the uncertain hope of morning
To make it to the shadows.
I'll die some anonymous day
And forever lament the sun, the songs,
The morning.
There's some truth
To that eternal hereafter,
My punishment will have begun.

Main Street Runs

*(Early summer sunrise, Main Street, Benton Harbor.
The date is irrelevant.)*

Silk thread rays
Of the morning sun
Stretch taut
From buildings and towers.
Cool pockets of early shadow
Yawn their contrast
From street to alley
Across the city.
Main Street runs
Its mausoleum corridor for blocks,
Running until it disappears
In the explosion of sunrise.

An aimless silhouette
Moves long and thin
Dragging a bent black body
Up the sidewalk.
He sings a raspy song,
His signal to other worlds
Wondering if there's life out there,
Lifting a brown paper bag
To silence his lips,
Waiting for an answer.

The Fountain

"Maids of the Mist" sit in silent bond
Observing us through a veil of spray
With children above and cherubs atop
Mischievously forcing the flow.
I sit a short distance away
Willing to share my bench
While memorizing the river,
Watching the channel for nothing
In particular, quietly trolling
For poetic grist.
The fountain spray arches to cascade
And splash around the stoic maidens,
Resounding like a thousand bare infant feet
Scurrying and slapping down a tiled hall.

I pass by on returning to other tasks,
Returning to earn my day, envious
Of maidens, children and cherubs,
Toying with a reincarnation of leisure
That would cast me as the eternal observer.

Mendel

*Performed at the opening of the Mendel Center for
Arts and Technology by American actor Sam Wanamaker*

No tired phoenix image this,
Rising now from a cursed shell
A Mendel starship to kiss
Satellites with signals.
The pulsing heart of technology pulls
Life from microchips. Downlinks
Give us eyes to the world.
A lamp to the future for those
With younger clothes.

I am business, touching
The commerce of Stuttgart.
I am a dreamer, touching
People of the Pacific Rim.
I am hope, learning
The lives of the Third World.
I am gentle, sobbing
Softly with actors and poets.
I am Mendel.

Theater to a global family
Building a community on the shore.
We sail fast into the 21st Century,
We will springboard minds that soar.

Falcon of knowledge nesting here.
Soft bird of wisdom gliding
With lasers of hard fact,
Flirting from behind the actor's masks

Of laughter and grief.
We are made whole, mind and emotions
As the future lives
In newborn tasks.
Cybernetic man braided to
Chambers of the heart;
Shadows of the soul.

We ride Edison's legacies
Into a new millenium.
Technoman will dance with symphonies,
Rest in the rapture of playwrights.
We are moving forward
As we rewrite Whitman in songs
Of our future selves.

Saigon on the Boulevard

*(There is a Vietnam Memorial that sits
on a bluff park in St. Joseph, Michigan)*

The land's edge runs a bluff park
Along the boulevard; a manicured
Strip of soft jade. The bluff
Standing sentry for centuries as
It gazes from the west bank
Over the great lake, where
The sand and sea witness
First loves, youthful lies,
Secret fears, quiet goodbyes.
And now they rest the pulse of
Hearts that have stopped beating.

The triangular pillar gouges up
From the hereafter, ripping through
The earth to slice skyward
In the coastal chill.
A proud and polished monument
To service. A medal of remembrance
For the scars of sadness.

Another granite hostage of war
To reflect faces that won't forget.
Faces that free fine moist lines
Of sorrow a few times each year.
Those special days when women
And men sob from coast to coast
In a thousand parks by a thousand
Monuments for thousands from
A single generation. Knowing
Tears are the only holy water.

Presidents and the Pentagon
Took us all to Vietnam.

54

A Gulf of Tonkin resolution
From those in Congress shouting loudest.
The young then made their contribution,
Fathers arguing over who was proudest.

A young soldier lies with dimming eyes
Looking up from a torso with no legs,
Feebly stuffing his crimson entrails
Back from where they came, asking
Someone to help him to his feet.

The gauze of misty twilight
Veils the last helicopter gunship.
It lifts off to hang suspended,
Vulture-like on a gnarled branch
Of history. It rises now from
The forest floor, a brief clearing
Created confidently from a New Testament
Book; the gospels according to
Agent orange and napalm.

A meaningless nose-tilt nod,
A quick swingturn to starboard
And the copter aims dead center
Into an oversized apricot orb
That is a southeast Asian sunset.

Why doesn't the sound fade away?
The spinning chopper blades offer
Their staccato chant of chooka-
Chooka-chooka-chooka, caromming
Off of naked trees
And broken dreams
To echo never, never,
NEVER AGAIN!

DEDICATION

The author was born and raised in Berrien County, Michigan. "Saigon on the Boulevard" is dedicated to the following people who were from that county and who never returned from Vietnam.

Ernest Watson
Bruce L. Marosites
Edward C. Sexton
William R. Roussos
Larry D. Butgereit
David L. Berkholz
John T. Wetzel
Lamarre A. Major
Robert L. Linn. Jr.
Charles E. Fletcher
Michael C. Farrell
Doyle L. Harris
Ricky L. Herndon
Jay B. Martine, Jr.
Johnnie W. Kelley
Wendell G. Vaughn
James G. Edinger
Thomas P. Pruiett, Jr.
Donald F. Wood
Carl T. Murdock
Frank E. Williams
Roger D. Shafer
Roy N. Uedler
Larry F. Hoadley

James R. Pruett
Willie S. Davis
Eugene Crossley
Philip A. Johnson
Gerald Przybylinski
Dale L. Johnson
William M. Treadway
Allan W. Persicke
Timothy A. Cook
John R. Vinnedge
James E. Townley, Sr.
Richard A. Brueck
Bobby G. Haney
James W. Lindemann
Richard L. Van De Warker
Carl D. Dixon
Randall A. Carver
Thomas H. Herndon
Jerry M. Weaver
Gary L. Ruff
James A. Wells
Gregory W. Hermann
Laurence E. Froehlich

Distance Runners

Take the mark for
Distant horizons
Lying beyond veiled vision.

Life's broad beach unrolls
Out of sight beside ripped
Meandering bluffs,

Cliffs reaching high
To glare at the battle
Between sand and sea.

Phantom heroes
Stand crystallized
On the high ground,

Dust-covered monuments
Magnified by time. Tides
Devour our path, our prints.

Arrogant waves argue
Over our epitaph.
We steal moments

To mold our warmth,
Spilling love on the beach
As we run naked into the sun.

Daily Paper

The early morning paper
Gives kinship with the world
As your coffee cup drains
Your eyes drink in the news.

Nations grasp for a piece of time
Reaching for a dim reflection.
Millions starve in silent corners;
Uniforms march to the sobs
Of countless, trembling mourners.

Warriors
And beggars
Serve their king
In fateful brotherhood.

Important to know
For pretentious minds
And mothers who will forget
How to sleep for awhile.

Fear and apathy
Take you past the legacies
To a baseball pitcher's 20 wins,
To a Peanuts and his friends.
Lucy waits to touch your mind
Psychological help
    for a dime.

When Fate is the Only Mentor

Nothing I do passes time,
Captive to a clock and fear.
Oh, to be an asbestos giant
Able to pluck the sky's eye or
Pinch it out to urge the night.
(Maybe I'd juggle it between
The horizons)
Fear preys on finite frailty;
Shadowy hawk stalking
To swoop us up, threatening
Some ill-defined demise.

Church service makes me nervous,
Paul Simon and I agree, but
I'm only really afraid
In hospitals and
In love.
Thank you for the confident words.
Didn't help but your caring does
When fate is the only mentor,
As in hospitals and
In love.

It'll be a joke when it's over.
Will you lie down with me now?
You are all that makes time pass.
I wait for tomorrow so I can laugh
At yesterday.

Territorial Road
and Other Sorrows

His brother was killed
In the crazy side
Of the city,
The side that seems
To be winning.
His shattered skull
Saving metal slugs
For coroners and morticians.
I didn't know him.
He was a brother to my friend;
Friendship is enough
For sorrow.

The father's anger
Tracked the animal
To return the madness,
Rescued from his rage
By my friend,
Stealing grief's victim.

He performed the act himself
In primeval assurance
Of justice.
They've locked my friend away.
He told me of possessions
That have always been his
And ours.
We hold them dear,
Our vengeance
And our love.

Live From Baskin-Robbins

Comradery accompanies the crackling
Of cones in the out-of-place place
Among girdered monuments from which
Patrons anxiously come.
Suits, sweatshirts, bare feet, wingtips
Congregate to contemplate a choice.
A strange exchange of licking
And laughing when a glance is a smile
Where ice cream is shared.

Small crowds leave through a
Bell-harnessed door, turning their backs.
They take their paths while
Carrying cones into summer heat
Where ice cream melts away.

Beach Grass

Tanned billows of
Flowing sand lie
Festooned between slight dunes
Frocked by sporadic beach grass.

Thread-like beach grass
Waves up at rustling cottonwoods,
Fans resting gulls,
Beckons you advance
With slender fingers.

Beach grass anchors strong
Against wind and winter and tide,
Holding the beige carpet of coast
As nature's legacies are refortified.

The shifting margin of sand
Spreads its defiance,
Offering no escort
Through the rising
Quivering heat.

You are stronger than you know,
You'll find forces in hidden places.
Tremors, tragedies and tears
Are teachers. It's how we learn
Of earthquakes and heartbreaks,
It's how we get a soul.

Leave the brink
For distant unseen someones
Calling across the bank.
Scorn the heat
And go slow so
You don't miss them.

Love Ride

Your satin breath anoints me
With a velvet tongue
Mapping a gentle path
From my lips
To brush my neck,
My chest.
The ribbon of your warmth
Gift-wraps life
Between darkness and dawn.

In the midnight sounds
I rise with the essence
Of your movement
To join in the soft journey
Through night air,
Sharing a love ride
To the morning sun.

Sunrise

The alarm and life
Pull me up again
to watch for your
Squinting and blinking
Over the eastern ridge.
We take our peek together
In the early day,
Looking over the landscape
To a tune of whether
It's worth it.

You'll rise out of your
Furtive glance at today
To stare at me—us.
You always do.
We both know you're
No freer than I.

You drop shimmering threads
That are grabbed and tied
To invisible hope,
Or a gallows beam.
Huddled groups dangle
Suspended from the end
Of your nylon line.
Dangling groups with a
Death-tight grip and a
Hope that fate is benign.

DATE DUE
